Watermarks

Poems

Julie Chappell

Watermarks

Cover design: Rowan Kehn
Book Design: Rowan Kehn

ISBN: 979-8-9868994-8-0

Turning Plow Press

In memory of my father, Gordon 'Dale' Chappell, Sr. an unknown artist, even though he could draw any image free hand, paint with oils, watercolors, and acrylics on canvas, craft jewelry, and create wood carvings. His artistic efforts were always given to family and friends freely, and with love.

This book is dedicated to my best friend, my husband, and the love of my life, Hank Jones

Contents

Life, Love, and the Pursuit **11**

Haiku for Hank...5
Hit is not al gold that glareth. 6
Nature's palette...7
Reflections...8
As I pirouette away redux 9
The scent of lilacs up the road 10
Juniper berry eaters 11
Sounds of evening coming on.............................12
Forest symphony...13
Philomela 14
His shadow knows 15
Osage Copperhead.......................................16
The Wasp..17
Hummingbird Wars 18
Reynard's offspring.......................................19
The Snake Charmer 20
Sun on strike 21
The rich get rich and the poor get poorer.....................22
The Saga of the Curly-tailed Lizards 23
Hazardous Hokey, Perilous Pokey 24
The spirits of your ancestors remain 25
Generations...26
Whistle while we work....................................28
Stirring my tea..29
Departures..30
In your den...31
Visions on tile while sitting on porcelain.................32
What is honour? A word. What is in that word honour?.......33
An unpretentious life 34
Futility 35
Christmas Ghosts..36
Lost in time 37
Love in the days of desperation 38

Venus was a Man...**39**

Venus was a man..41
Venus, her confidante..42
The *Anemoi*..43
On the bones of the Romans.......................................44
Tales from the Earth...45
Holy static..46
The double sorwe of Troilus to tellen..........................47
Remembrances...48
Who's There?...49
Listening to a reading of Pope's introduction to *Iliad*.........50
No empty vessel this...52
Origin of a corrosive species....................................53
Why that is an avisioun..55
Drab divinity..56
Spinning Jesus...57
Divine meet-cute...58
Neutrino...59

I

Life, Love, and the Pursuit

Honeysuckle blooming, never dormant
Swallows nesting, rebuilding
Mauve roses blossoming, glorious
Russian sage greening, growing
Iris stalks standing, shoots popping
Bushes flowering, leafing
Red roses loading thorny branches
Rose of Sharon, the late bloomer
tempus fugit from us all.

Haiku for Hank

Pretty yellow butterfly
gone before I can
speak these words.

Hit is not al gold that glareth.
        Chaucer, *The House of Fame*, l. 272

The greed of the goldfinch
belies his brilliant hue,
shining like gold in the sun.

He gobbles and spews and
wreaks havoc on his kind coming
to break their own fast each morning.

Nature's palette

Bright red cardinal
alight
in bare trees

Dull red squirrels
jumping
limb to limb

Blue Jay calling
mimicking
avian cries

Black cat watching
defying
laws of gravity

Brown raccoon squinting
waiting
for darkness to fall

Dusty grey opossum
scurrying
blind to all.

Reflections

The placid surface of the lake at dusk
reflects the skeletons of winter trees,
the droughty earth framing lake and rocks,
a discarded garment, ragged but whole.

Pelicans float and fly across the surface
their reflections growing dim in the fading
twilight, the mirroring surface remaining calm,
life and death gliding above and below its gleam.

In all the spaces of this Garden, humans
pervert their own reflections with artificial mirrors,
to deny their mortality, their bankrupt natures
discarding garments, ragged and unholy.

As I pirouette away redux

My morning dance with the spiders has changed
in a summer of drought after a spring of plenty.

There are still webs to clear with careful precision,
still arabesques and balancé to master as I go along.

But now, there are only small spiders, tiny, perfect webs,
unlike Halloween imitations of string and plastic when

we trick or treat ourselves with alien monstrous beings
and adorn our dwellings with faux spiders and their webs

that alive would scare us half to death, sending chills
like spidery legs slithering along every vessel of our bodies.

As I twist, spin, and hold my breath, de-webbing with
thoughts of spiders dancing in my head, I recall gargantuan

wolf spiders last year waiting patiently on the ceiling above our
heads to catch smaller morsels wandering oblivious.

Once, prolific giant arachnids webbed our doors shut, trapping
us inside, to signify *our* natural habitat.

Now, tiny grey spiders twirl webs each night creating spidery
byways that by morning I must pirouette away.

The scent of lilacs up the road

The scent of lilacs up the road in Spring
enticed the child I was to beg the gift of one
fragrant bundle growing on the bush that
thrived on the land of our closest neighbor.

They must have planted that bush long before
I drew breath, learned to walk, to plead for
the purest fragrance and delicate beauty
floating on a sturdy stalk of wood.

These lilacs of my childhood emblematic
of a time when we regarded each other
even tended each other's young sprouts
with watchful eyes and better, kinder hearts.

When that lilac bush bloomed in May,
my birth month, the child I was believed
it bloomed for me, a girl enraptured
by the sweetest scent she'd ever know.

These lilacs of my childhood are gone now,
like my childhood once imbued with such
simple pleasures and gentle neighbors, only
to be revived in memory and poetry.

Juniper berry eaters

A little goldfinch plucks juniper berries
off the tree outside my study window
as if his life depends upon these tiny, blue spheres.

And so it may, in spite of two hanging feeders
dutifully filled where he and his fellows queue
in nearby trees fighting incessantly for position.

These winter goldfinches, sleek and shining
in muted golds, greens, and black carry the
vulgar stamp of "non-breeding" males.

Does that mean that the juniper-berry eater
and his fellows are a goldfinch order of *castrati*
snipped by Nature for population control?

And that these boy birds are bestowed with more
beautiful songs sung in high ecstatic voices
bolstered by the consuming of juniper berries?

Or is it only that the throes of winter defrock their
brilliant hues of yellow breast and black wings to
drabber shades anointing them seasonal monks?

My imagination betrays an anthropomorphizing
search for solace in the life of other creatures
inspired by Nature rather than by a Janus-faced god.

Sounds of evening coming on

I

A squirrel complains bitterly about wrongdoing
while his tormentors fly coolly away
filling the air with their victory caws.

II

Wind howls and water churns red-brown
with foamy, whitecapped tops like tanks
rolling over a muddy, bloody battlefield.

III

The twilight stillness of a forest in repose
settling, quieting, calming our essence soon
undone by Man ejaculating with his gun.

Forest symphony

On a warm, golden autumn afternoon
I try to tease out an opening to a story
of violent, mysterious death, unlikely
villains swirling through my brain.

But the chickadees keep twittering (real tweets)
and the tufted titmice chitter at each other,
at the chickadees, at the squirrels, at me
forcing me to listen carefully to the sounds

of real life, of play, of survival of the swiftest,
and I cannot hear their musical accompaniment
without feeling alive, feeling grateful for being
allowed to become a single note in their symphony.

Philomela

The red-gold leaves of the late autumn oak
reflect the afternoon sun like ancient mirrors
made for the workmen in Egyptian tombs,
only the antique leaves lay above ground, and I,
alive, drift from thought to thought finding it
impossible to hold one still long enough to
consider or create or contemplate beyond the
chittering, twittering, chirruping sounds
twirling my thoughts in glorious circles

until *avis*-like

I fly among the rustling leaves of a Pin Oak
then into the crisper, mud-reds of a Blackjack
spinning, spiraling, buoyant, floating free
on wings of my own imagining.

His shadow knows

I hear his feet on the rooftop before
I see his shadow flitting across the leaves
of the tree opposite, as if his shadow's making
practice runs before the living creature
makes the leaps and bounds he must
to gain purchase on a tree nearby
to thrive, to fly in sweet surrender.

If only our shadows could practice in
leaps and bounds and end-runs on life
before we make the jump from age to age
to gain purchase on each one before it's gone
to thrive, to fly in sweet surrender.

Osage Copperhead (*Agkistrodon contortrix phaeogaster*)

The snake inlaid with copper skin
steals my complacent days and nights
reminds me of human vulnerability
as he lies quietly in wait for my
next performance of primal fear.

Such astounding Beauty and Grace
we must and cannot live with in peace
and whether shovel or hoe divides him
from his life, his awe- and fear-inspiring
presence menaces every step I take.

The Wasp

The wasp, a mud dauber, stretches
her shapely body, extending graceful legs
performing ballet steps on the glass
—plié, pirouette, arabesque—her 'toes'
carefully pointed in fifth position as she
moves her legs up and down keeping her
'knees' crossed with ease until her 'arms'
begin to wave around, up, and over her
body, her head, her antennae, when she
suddenly stops all movement and begins
to step in slow motion, walking ever so
elegantly up the window glass to the
beveled edge of this, her stage, where
she turns, takes a few careful steps, bows,
then disappears into the wings
waiting for her encore.

Hummingbird Wars

I carefully measure out the refined sugar
and test the heat of the water for melting same.

I whisk and whisk without cease until the tiny
grains of sweetness disburse themselves invisible.

I follow the simple recipe to create safe, enticing
nectar for our one, lone hummingbird.

I hang the tiny mason jar feeder with its four,
red, faux flower portals and wait and watch.

I hear the consequent whir of tiny wings and
see the approach, the first sip, sweetness and bird united.

Delighted and comforted that my offering is acceptable
to this tiny god of the forest, I sigh and turn, but

more whirring and a thud sends my eyes spinning
trying to focus on the sipper just there or there or there?

Not one. Not two. Not three. But four tiny gods now at war.

Transfixed, fascinated, horrified to see
four, tiny, ruby-throated hummers in battle

over imagined boundaries, like all living things,
these gorgeous creatures fashioned by Nature for war.

Reynard's offspring

Our resident grey fox kits
frolic freestyle, fretless,
skulk, stroll, scrounge,
stare, streak, and thieve.

Their brazen cuteness striding
under or across our deck
making free and easy, ever
hopeful that we'll relent,

that we won't keep shooing,
stifling, standing guard against
these two interloping beauties

so to protect, pet, and pamper
a smaller, gentler soul who has
adopted us as his own, a black cat,

our Harry, once abandoned in the forest,
unwanted, untended, unprotected,
left to fend alone in a place where

raccoons act out their natures,
skulking, scrounging, and scheming
while opossums furtively do the same,

where these adorable, persistent kits
try to avoid growing up for a little longer
like most offspring in this postmodern age.

The Snake Charmer

for Walter Bargen

The snake writhes a bit in his hands
before calming, responding to the man's
easy, gentle grip, end to end before
he settles the snake within a specially
prepared painter's bucket designed
to save both man and snake from suffering.

Snake and bucket now nestled firmly
into a handmade wooden frame in the
front seat of the car, the man drives with
one eye on the road and one on the bucket,
hoping for a smooth and gentle ride.

The man and the snake arrive intact to
a wildlife preserve where the man gingerly
lifts the bucket up and out of the frame
slowly carrying it to the muddy riverbank.

The man's 20th capture and release, the snake's 1st,
his kind, if not his kin – 15 rattlers, 4 copperheads –
preceding him on this journey, with this man,

the Northern Water snake, unconscious of its status,
slithers away to freedom, the man, wishing he could do the
same.

Sun on strike

The sun went into hiding this morning
refusing to appear, to burn off the darkness.

Sun is tired of being blamed
for overheated, toxic air, for ending lives.

"You did this to Earth," Sun cries out.
"You and no other living thing, just YOU!"

The rich get rich and the poor get poorer
In the meantime, in between time
Ain't we got fun?
              Raymond B. Egan and Gus Kahn, (1921)

10 AM

Three people in a stolen car
Rob a discount store.
The chase is on.

News helicopter flies overhead.
Caravan of cops and robbers ensues
Heads west to the woods and the lake.

Police tactical error sends them and
Perps spinning in the wrong lane
Shots fired. None find purchase.

Stolen car dumped in the woods
K-9 unit can't see the forest for the trees.
Police marine unit on call, baffled.

Woods thick and hellishly hot
Residents told to stay inside,
So they go out lickety-split.

6 PM

Two locals spot the baddies, alert police.
Joyriding robbers, two jailed, defiant,
One hospitalized, dehydrated.

Police and news folk wrap up their gear.
Residents' go inside, their 5-minutes secure.
Human drama finished. Forest liberated.

The Saga of the Curly-tailed Lizards

The snow started falling in large, wet flakes
onto my windshield, on the concrete of
the parking lot outside the pet store where I sat,
one winter morning, waiting to buy crickets.

My son, turning 10 that year, had two
curly-tailed lizards residing in a large
aquarium, filled with sand, driftwood, and
various rocks, atop an antique chest.

He acquired the lizards from a neighbor boy
who lived one week at his mother's, across the street,
and one week at his father's, in another part of the city,
one of whom gave the order to bestow his lizards elsewhere.

We kept Ruby and Lily alive and well until
I finished grad school, and we were moving away, so
back to that pet store, supplier of crickets, to return the lizards,
but, sadly, never back to their desert home.

You do the hokey pokey
And you turn yourself around
That's what it's all about.
          Larry LaPrise, *"The Hokey Pokey,"* (1948)

Hazardous Hokey, Perilous Pokey

Her left foot slides out from under layered
bedcovers overwarm, confined, seeking freedom
while her right foot nestles more temperate within.

She wriggles the left foot to test the air, the right
remaining snug, her body still in a strange half-life
as the furnace roars to life to justify the right.

She tumbles half in half out of manic dreams
and wonders if the sound of her cats is real
or if their mewling whimperings only dreams.

As consciousness rises raising reality rightly, and
she hears the eternal winds of Oklahoma nipping,
ripping the last winter leaves off trees, spinning

swirling the fallen into tornadoes of decaying dust
as the Blue Jay turns cuckoo in a foreign nest,
the sweet, brown wren anxiously cries out to his mate.

Spring advances to dislodge unrepentant Winter,
angered at imagined slights, killing buds and tiny
nestlings, caught in the crossfire of warring factions.

The spirits of your ancestors remain

I was talking to my grandparents just now.
Although they are no longer in this world,
I like to contemplate chats of long ago

before I moved too far away in time and place
to sit by their graves, side by side, joined across
from those of my mother's and father's.

If you can't talk to the spirits of your ancestors
who can you talk to, who knows you better,
knows your affective heart, your chastened soul?

If you can't talk to the spirits of your ancestors
must you wait until you die to do so and hope
that in that afterlife you all can have a chat?

If you can't talk to the spirits of your ancestors
how do you know who you were, who you are,
who you have been when your body fades away?

If you can't talk to the spirits of your ancestors
how do you live each day in the desecration of
the world, in the throes of disaffection, war, sorrow?

I was talking to my grandparents just now telling them
how much I miss them and will miss them for all time,
my spirit hoping to be missed and talked with in its turn.

Generations

At 16, we always drove
to Allen's Drive-In
after school to see and be seen
before time called us home
to homework, chores, and family.

Dropped off at my gate
I walked up the path
into the old farmhouse
expecting to smell sweet
or savory scents of supper to come.

But that day no scent of freshly
baked bread, of cookies, of a meal,
no promising aromas greeted me.
Only a note on the table—
"Grandma fell and is in the hospital."

My grandmother couldn't walk,
step, jump, run, turn, or dance.
How could she fall sitting in
her wheelchair, reading, crocheting
complaining to my mother?

But that day, the phone began to ring
and my mother left her mother waiting
to be moved from wheelchair to toilet.
"Wait," my mother said, moving away,
her mother, never patient, moved anyway.

The accidental nature of grandmother's
fall insufficient to assuage the guilt
long-placed in my mother's conscience,
exacerbated by her mother's bodily affliction
neither quietly nor patiently suffered by either.

Whistle while we work

My mother's whistling song filled
our house while she made food, cleaned up,
tended her mother, her husband, her children.

She whistled classical, bebop, and
rock and roll, forcing any darkness away.

I learned to recreate her whistle but
not her domestic endeavors.

My main labors – reading, writing, teaching –
fed my children, our critters, and me while

making food, cleaning up, tending to all,
took a backseat as domestic endeavors.

Still, I whistled classical, bebop,
rock and roll, drawing off the darkness
her song now my own.

Stirring my tea

I slowly stirred the sugar into
my steaming cup of tea and heard
my mother doing the same, only

she's been gone from the earth
for a long time now and had no
tea in the last painful years of life.

I have stirred sugar into tea before
without hearing the echo of my mother
as I did just now, this minute, as if

she is here guiding my motion,
stirring my brew with practiced hand
soothing me with her gentle, loving touch.

Departures

My mother claimed my father flew into the room,
said goodbye and flew out the closed window

when he died that afternoon in the room next to
where she would lay her head each night.

She had been sitting in that room all day
talking with the widow of her dead brother.

My mother negotiating through a Parkinson's haze,
my aunt through her unrelenting Pollyanna gaze.

My day spent hovering over my dying father,
his unseeing eyes roving, sweat oozing from fever, fear?

He said only one word all day, as I wiped his sweat away,
"Don't!" he cried. I cried, "Daddy, Daddy!" but no reply.

My mother in that conjoined room told me that the hospice
worker smelled, had flies swarming all round him.

Was she, too, like my father at his dying, seeing the unseeable,
ghoulish figures conjured by fevered brains?

Did my father's spirit fly to my mother for one last kiss
as he departed their house, their life, our lives forever?

I'll be sure to ask him when I see him again hereafter.

In your den

We sat together in your den, me
watching you work your small vice
to secure a metal piece, for jewelry
you were making, you telling me
how proud you were of the story
I was working on for school.

Was it a story or a history essay?
Was I a sophomore or a junior in high school?
Was the jewelry you were making ring or earring?
Was that the day you told me that you gave up the job
you loved because your wife, my mother, couldn't cope?

Those details recede, elusive, untenable,
but your voice, your easy laughter, your artist's eye,
your fatherly comfort, never fade, but remain
secure in memory like hard metal locked in a vice.

Visions on tile while sitting on porcelain

I

At first the lovers' kiss, before a hiss
of snakes galore fills the floor until
the writhing evaporates revealing a
paleolithic painting the color of the Lascaux
wall but not of bull or horse, instead an early
dog-like creature leaps into the central panel
becoming a wolf howling at a full moon
then slowly consumed by a giant frog,
a baby stegosaurus watching beneath the
wings of a pterodactyl in determined flight.

II

The profile and elongated head of Nosferatu
morphed into the face of Mark Twain who
transformed into an ancient sea snail the sea
flowing up and around, rising into the
right leg and foot of a crucified Christ while
on the other side the sea billowed into the face
of an old crone whose hair became the top
of a dog's head the tip of its nose sniffing before
the swift movement of a donkey its head raised
brayed the news of the miracle of imagination.

III

Wolf howls at the full moon as Crow observes
her handiwork of twisted earth and roots turned Crown
above the ancient Nautilus shell with its eternal circles
and Crow flies to the world of men from treetop to treetop
crying her warning of what is to come.

What is honour? A word. What is in that word honour?
What is that honour? Air. A trim reckoning. Who hath it?
He that died o' Wednesday. Doth he feel it? No.
Doth he hear it? No. 'Tis insensible then? Yea, to the dead.
But will it not live with the living. No.

Falstaff, *1 Henry IV*, 5.1.133-37

As a child, I feared the darkness,
my brother filling my head with real
and imagined monsters of the night.

As an adolescent, I feared loneliness
Hollywood movies perverting my heart
with Romance not Reality.

As an adult, I feared failure in work
in family, not doing enough, being unworthy
the world filling my head with women's lacunae.

As I grew older, I feared dying too soon
or lingering in illness too long, a burden to
those I loved while death creeps ever closer.

As I near the end, I fear the consequences
of war raging night and day in a place where
real monsters invade, real loneliness abounds.

Worthy work upended by an unworthy tyrant leaving
lacunae in families and friends where men, women,
children fight against 'the murderous, cowardly pack.'

Today, I fear that along with disease, war, too, is
contagious as it rages here and there and everywhere
seeking meaningless Honor and Glory where neither exists.

An unpretentious life

I like this unpretentious life I lead
retired from the everyday.

No flashy cars or clothes
no conspicuous consumption.

I pad around my house, the cats'
Domestic, those unforgiving masters.

I write, I cook, I clean,
I read, I contemplate.

My days largely spent in
tasks of my own choosing.

Flashes of regret at what I didn't
or couldn't accomplish pass quickly.

Age has made certain of that—
regret being futile, unproductive.

The future, as for all creatures,
makes ready the same ending.

Futility

Watching my fingernails grow
long in a short span of time,
I wonder why?

Human hair and nails continuing
to grow after death, or shrinking
skin retreating from the hard keratin?

So am I dead, dying, or simply
slowly shrinking as my nails
grow long and lush to spite me?

Or is that a horror story replayed
in the films of our youth to
frighten us to mind our elders?

Or is it ritual body shaming to let
youth know theirs is a fleeting thing
the future decay of the body certain?

A *memento mori* for blood and bone.

Christmas Ghosts

Snow falling in Oxford in a movie
reminds me of a Christmas there
when not snow but rain poured heavily
under our umbrellas as we splashed
through puddles to find a quaint,
Polish restaurant with amazing food
accompanied by a lively duo playing
Christmas songs, singing in Polish
in that small, intimate space,
filled with warmth and light
on the eve before the Mass.

Lost in time

I prefer losing myself in the fourteenth century
to being stuck in a noisy, overburdened world.

You might wonder if I realize the dangers of that age
the murderous kings, the religious wars, the dread diseases.

Our age has them all in slightly altered form—
murderous despots, religious conflicts, and deadly diseases.

A veritable smorgasbord of disease plagues us now
Covid, Ebola, hantavirus, Lyme disease, multiple cancers.

Twenty-first century science can ease and save lives but cannot
stop the dread of disease or of political wrangling.

Cries of "pray for us, for them, for everyone" but why would a
god listen to the whims of arrogant human prayer?

Only love of kin and kind can save us now.

Love in the days of desperation

The van breaks down near the fateful Donner Pass.
Where the car sits unmoving, a rod for measuring snow rises
far above their heads.

Tow truck comes. She chooses to ride in the broken van with
her dogs and cats to ease all of their nerves as they fly along,
driverless, love for love.

Tin roof panels rust in splotches covering an outdoor bar.
Plastic walls shine, reflect, protect—those in or those out?
Fan blades quiet, sun slants, shadow threatens chill.
Some bored, some lost in time, some lost in faded love.

II

Venus was a Man

Mother of Rome, delight of Gods and men,
Dear Venus that beneath the gliding stars
Makest to teem the many-voyaged main
And fruitful lands — for all of living things
Through thee alone are evermore conceived,
Through thee are risen to visit the great sun
Before thee, Goddess, and they coming on.

Lucretius *De Rerum Natura*
(c. 50 BCE)

Venus was a man

A Carolingian cleric once preached
against the ignorance of the ancients'
belief in a panoply of deities in which,
he asserted, 'Venus was a man.'

He might have been on to something,
though never seeing in his world, wholly
dominated by images of god-like men,
statues of Venus, shapely female temptress.

Was his Latin weak, as Charlemagne declared,
or was the Latin masculine ending clear enough,
cohering as it did with Venus' mission to be
panderess of sexual love and longing?

Why not a man then? That beast of all beasts.
That other sinful creation thrown from the Garden.
After all, the Word was that the son of his god
was fully divine and fully human, a man indeed.

Where is your careless love gone to now . . .
While a lyre and Venus at night bring delight.
Ovid, *Heroides* 3.55, 129-30 (Tr. Harold Isbell)

Venus, her confidante

Young, perhaps 17, she would sit
upon her front porch, a small slab
of concrete and brick, to commune
with Venus aloft in the western sky.

Venus and she became intimate friends,
meeting each clear, summer night
to bemoan loves found and lost,
pangs of adolescent angst resounding.

Venus, mature and confident,
sure of her place in the universe.
She, adolescent and uncertain, sure
of nothing but Venus in the night sky.

And the frosts which are cruel when Boreas blows over the earth . . . across the
wide sea and stirs it up, while earth and the forest howl.
Hesiod, Works and Days (505-508)

And the gathering was stirred like the long sea-waves of the Icarian main, which
Euros or Notos has raised, rushing upon them from the clouds of father Zeus.
And even as when Zephyros at its coming stirreth the deep standing grain with its
violent blast, and the heads bow thereunder, even so was all their gathering stirred.
Homer, Iliad (2.144-49)

The *Anemoi*

Boreas blows a gale, a blast
across the water, whipping up
white caps, bending oaks to supplication.

Zephyros blows a gentle breeze,
barely rippling waters, setting
leaves adance in nascent green.

Notos blows a raging summer storm,
tears of rain blinding vision, senses,
whirlwinds of memories spinning away.

Euros blows spirits traveling along the verge
of lake and forest, lulls us into
a past, an unlooked-for respite, at last.

On the bones of the Romans

was just a line on a piece of paper
that floated by in her dream.
she couldn't read the other words,
the hand indecipherable except
for that one brief line

On the bones of the Romans

whose lineage we conflate deftly
moving backward from Claudius to Scipio,
who forged their blood road to Empire,
destroying and ravaging as they went.

The Carthaginians, the Gallic tribes,
Germania, Macedonia, Alexander's
bloody empirical progress that left Egypt
to Ptolemy to Cleopatra who succumbed to
Julius, Antony, Octavius, nasty, grasping boys.

Bloody Romans, blood of the Romans

from Britannia to Mesopotamia, Dacia to Africa,
the Roman army laid waste, rebuilding in its own image.
Conquest instead of Compassion.
Colonies instead of Communities.

Veni, vidi, vici, proclaimed the bastard of Rome.

These were her thoughts waking in the dark of night,
destruction and chaos reverberating throughout.

Tales from the Earth

A dropped, jet rosary bead
at the site of an abbey in the
demolition deposit tells a story—

perhaps of a nun, sent away from
her house by Henry VIII's faithless minions,
dropping her beads as the King's agents push
her along, not allowed to retrieve a symbol of *her* faith.

Evidence of Iron Age trackways around an
East Riding chariot burial, well before the
Romans arrived to dominate, to orient all
along their crafty, well-crafted roads.

Fragments of a pysse pot at Hampton Court
the remnants of the last go of courtier or conspirator
apissing in the night leaving his mark for all time
in the bottom of a ceramic pot but nowhere else.

Holy static

They told me it was *only* scintillating scotomas
offering a light show, like those Hildegarde of Bingen
believed brought personal messages to her from God.

The only messages I get from God come via lacerating
radio static caused by a too-near Christian station proclaiming
"institute....God....avoid burn....Hell....sign up....Money."

Backing out of my driveway, I clear the ungodly static,
locating Mozart, Beethoven, Vivaldi, Handel, Bach,
gods of ethereal notes, tonal melody, rapturous chords.

Hildegarde, mistress of her own music soaring beyond
plainsong, beyond those celebrated male masters, her song
created in her own name while wrapped in *spiritus dei.*

The double sorwe of Troilus to tellen,
That was the kyng Priamus sone of Troye,
In lovynge, how his aventures fellen
From wo to wele, and after out of joie.
        Chaucer, *Troilus and Criseyde* (c. 1382)

Every ancient love story blames the woman—
for the failure of love by woman's lustful nature,
they tell us of her unquenchable desires leading men astray,
rendering them weak, weeping, raging for revenge, for war.

Eve offering god-like wisdom from His own creature
eats the forbidden fruit, shares it with her man, who,
unquestioning, eats what she offers, but it is Eve
who suffers pain, enmity, and forced submission to Man.

Helen, product of the rape of her mother, Leda, by the Greek
god Zeus, bears the blame for her own *raptus*
by Paris, prince of Troy, for the great war, Helen suspected,
too, of lusting after the ever-guiltless Hector.

Pandora, Medea, Delilah, Clytemnestra, Guenevere,
Criseyde, Lady Macbeth, Bertha Mason, Emma Bovary
Nora Helmer, Scarlett O'Hara, Sula, Olive Kitteridge,
a never-ending list of bad girls to justify patriarchal power.

Remembrances

At the end of each day, Thomas Cromwell
always noted what needed doing the next day,
his Remembrances—who to arrest, imprison,
extort money or property from, whose ass to
kick, whose ass to kiss, the villain always
belying the genius, the rational thinker,
the vicegerent of spirituals to the king of corruption.

We common folk make to-do lists that remind
us to—wash the car, water the plants, clean the
house/garage/closet/shed, pay the bills, visit
the dentist/doctor/counselor/teacher, a host of
necessary reminders in this ordinary,
irrational world, spirituality optional.

In his turn as sycophant to the mad Tudor monarch
Cromwell finally lost his own head. Remembrances
no longer needed when the head is separated, spitted
like a piece of meat on a skewer and set out for
public consumption.

We common folk may lose our heads metaphorically,
trying to make ends meet when the ends are too far apart,
remembering all the tasks, duties, obligations of each day,
struggling with spiritual wranglings within ourselves.

We who are unnecessary to the grander schemers' and their
self-serving missions, remain obscured—but whole.

Who's There?

Hamlet sees a ghost
(extremely ungodly thing to do)

Hamlet commands Ophelia to get to a nunnery
(convent or brothel?)

Hamlet seeks revenge
(inspired not by a god but by a ghost?)

Hamlet suffers righteous indignation
(mommy issues unresolved)

Hamlet cries, "there's more in Heaven and Earth, Horatio"
(failing to elaborate)

Hamlet double blinds Rosencrantz and Guildenstern (assassins'
fools)

Hamlet kills Polonius who's doubly blind
(by arras and sycophancy)

Hamlet blind to mother's culpability in Ophelia's murder
(Horatio aiding Mommie Dearest?)

Hamlet reacts violently to Ophelia's death
(after talking to the skull of a King's jester)

Hamlet draws his sword against Laertes
(a man spied on by his father, tricked by his King)

Hamlet dies pleading with Horatio to tell his story
(a Christ complex left to a Judas-like man).

Listening to a reading of Pope's introduction to *Iliad*

Poetry to prose to poetry in prose

Dissonance occurs as I listen to a recording on the e-platform called YouTube of a reading (2016) of Alexander Pope's introduction to his translation (1713) of Homer's epic poem, *Iliad* (750BCE), Homer's alleged history of the Trojan war (1177BCE) on the fertile plains of Asia Minor by the forces of Sparta, Mycenae, and allies, warriors of the Mediterranean world against the treasure hoarding, horse-breakers of Ilium, a war occurring some 500 years before Homer sang his song, recounting the *raptus* of the wife of the Spartan king, whose *xenia*, whose Honor was negated by a prince of Troy, to be avenged only through violent acts of war perpetrated upon young and old, women and children, dying at the hands of heroes and villains alike.

Pope introduces this translation proclaiming, "Skepticism is as much the result of knowledge as knowledge is of skepticism." A bold and yet confounding statement at the beginning of the eighteenth-century as of the twenty-first. Is the current skepticism about science the result of knowledge? Is the current knowledge of science the result of skepticism? The answer to the former must be a resounding NO while the answer to the latter must be YES. Pope's assertion in the second decade of the 1700s may have been defensible among his class but in the third decade of the 2000s in the face of socioeconomic derangement and a plague for all ages, it is not.

Pope concurs, "To be content with what we at present know, is, for the most part, to shut our ears against conviction; since from the very gradual character of our education, we must continually forget, and emancipate ourselves from knowledge previously acquired; we must set aside old notions and embrace fresh ones; and, as we learn, we must be daily unlearning something which it has cost us no small labour and anxiety to acquire." That is the rub which signals the essence of our social distress in the 2020s, as our society crumbles, as knowledge and skepticism blur and fail to fuel each other, people staunchly entrenched on either side of an impossible dialectic.

Pope asks in regard to his subject, Homer, "which theory or theories" (about great writers and their contributions to society) should we choose? Pope claims that "Homeric knowledge may be described as a free permission to believe any theory, provided we throw overboard all written tradition." I would assert a similar vein of thought, replacing "Homeric knowledge" with scientific knowledge as Science currently attempts to unpick ways to alleviate the plague that ravages bodies and minds. The volumes of competing theories, not Science, but spreading like the virus itself, fragment a society enslaved to electronic devices carried on our bodies like sacred books, giving us agency unearned to cherry pick theories that collude with our individual and collective ignorance and shut our ears against the truth of the words.

Scientia is knowledge. *Skepsis* is doubt. *Doubt* is fear.

Come into the garden, Maud,
For the black bat, night has flown,
Come into the garden, Maud,
I am here at the gate alone;
And the woodbine spices are wafted abroad,
And the musk of the rose is blown.

Alfred Lord Tennyson, *Maud*, 1854

No empty vessel this

She stands by the lake glowing
in the rays of a setting sun
as fireflies flicker in the fading light.

She turns from the water knowing
the coldness of his heart, hard as stone,
as scorpions lurk in the night.

She walks up the hill bestowing
a glance back to her shadow alone,
as foxes watch out of sight.

She sighs into the wind blowing
her anguished cry across the water,
as men skulk away from doing right.

Origin of a corrosive species

On a cold, snowy morning plants of various sorts
sit in pots along the stone wall of my window sill
warm and well-tended inside, they seem to be staring
with envy at the cold, snow-covered junipers and oaks
in the forest on the other side of the glass, reaching for
the sun far above the house, Russian sage, pineapple,
bonsai, money tree sigh for their kin but not their kind.

The Russian sage wishing to change its origins now
wishing it were not from the Steppes of Central Asia
its native land synonymous with unprovoked aggression,
tyranny, and prevarication of the most despicable sort.
The beauty of its deeply purple flowers and aromatic leaves
may have inspired poets of its homeland to breathe deeply
before they felt compelled to dissident lines, proclaiming
cruelties, injustices, genocides, in Holodomor, in Kyiv.

The pineapple, now symbol of the paradisal islands, first
growing and sweetening for the Mayans and Aztecs around the
time that Homer recorded epic warriors sacrificing their own
blood and that of other creatures for calm seas to prevail in a
ten-year unwinnable war, most were lost while
a few sailed away for home only to be seduced to be playthings
of those same gods wallowing in sacrificial blood, corpses
staining their altars while peace-loving Mayans disappeared and
war-mongering Aztecs made blood sacrifice with purple corn,
papayas, and pineapples.

The bonsai leaves touch the glass, seeking their true height and
breadth, miniaturized by humans trying to grasp the sacred in
concentrated spaces, a hundred years before the holy prophet
Muhammad sought his divinity through sacred voices and
visions purported to be from the Archangel Gabriel sending
the Prophet traveling from Mecca to Jerusalem to pray in good
company, ever after the followers of all those praying together
at Al-Aqsa disseminating disparate messages retuned over the

ages to notes of power as they killed each other making their own sacrifices and corpses, full lives for miniatures.

The money tree spreads its deep green leaves, long and wide, while thick separate trunks twine and twist round each other to become one, harmonious, brought to this land, not its homeland, by the most inharmonious ungodly pilgrims bringing with the money plant their diseases, killing and maiming, so they could claim the land god-given to them, an angry god no indigenous could comprehend and on went the pilgrim-like folk from land to land in search of money trees that bloomed gold or shed dollars, shekels, dinars, sterling, francs, marks, rubles, blood, sweat, tears, divesting the colonized of culture, of religion, of life.

Why that is an avisioun
And this a revelacioun,
Why this a drem, why that a sweven,
And nought to every man liche even.
          Chaucer *The House of Fame I.7-10*

I

Clown white paper and greasepaint swirl
while the dog pees on the carpet in a half-lit room
and a writer lies half conscious, in half sleep, wondering
avisioun or *revelacioun, consolatio* or *mundus inversus?*

II

My sweet dog died years ago
I never used greasepaint
The child I was feared clowns,
The masquerade disguising nothing.

III

Macrobius might see *visio* in the empty white paper
proof of a writer's fears that no words will come,
while neither *solas* nor *sentence* succors a world in need
and the writer, wordless, idles in her own solipsistic whirl.

Drab divinity

The drab beige outer structure
inspires nothing but a sense of
the drab beige religion lurking within,

offering worn out platitudes, attitudes
of hell-fire and devotion to the
Master Manipulator so you must

get gathered up with the rest of
the sheep to be trussed up tight
as an offering but not to the Divine

rather, to human greed and power
of the merest kind ever ready to
destroy divinity indefinitely.

Spinning Jesus

Jesus spins his body down the hill,
long, dark hair flying out around his head

no ancient sistrum rattles or trumpet blasts
only drum, bass, and voice urge him on

as he keeps spinning toward the pond
where we are sure he will cross undrowned

our acid-tangled minds mesmerized
in silent reckoning of his relentless reality.

Divine meet-cute

Jesus, Buddha, Mohammed, and The Baru sit
in deep discussion on an ancient stone
in the Garden of Earthly Delights.

Anansi the spider descends slowly
on his shining thread above their heads.

Chufi the rabbit watches surreptitiously
munching grass near their feet.

Reynard the Fox flits slyly tree to tree
cunningly listening to their talk.

Sun Wukong the monkey shapeshifts
as he comes near the stone.

Their presence peopling the Garden
while the prophets posture in perpetuity.

Yonder see the morning blink:
  The sun is up, and up must I,
To wash and dress and eat and drink
And look at things and talk and think
  And work, and God knows why.

A.E. Housman, *Last Poems: XI (1922)*

Neutrino

a particle lighter than an electron
nearly invisible, passes through earth
unimpeded by solid matter.

If only humans could be lighter
nearly invisible, to pass through earth
unimpeded by irrational matter.

Neutrino

fundamental to all the processes
of the universe, nearly 97%
of the whole, incomprehensible.

If only humans could be fundamental
not detrimental to a universe to which
we are wholly incomprehensible.

Neutrino

electrically neutral in its composition,
its evolution from place to place
remaining undetectable.

If only humans could be electrically neutral
in composition, in evolution,
remaining undetectable.

Acknowledgments

I am grateful to the following for publishing my creative aspirations:

Invited Poet Interviewee. *Spotlighting Oklahoma: Oral History Project*. Oklahoma State University Library, Interviewer: Emily Blackshear. Oklahoma Oral History Research Program. Oklahoma State University, April 14, 2021. Recording/transcript published in 2023.

"Origin of a corrosive species" first published in *Walt Whitman Two Hundred and Five: A Poetry Anthology for Walt Whitman's 205th Birthday*, ed. James P. Wagner, New York: Local Gems Poetry Press, 2024.

"Visions on tile while sitting on porcelain" first published in *Equinox*, Vol. 7, Houston, TX, Fall 2024.

Many thanks to the organizers at the following venues for inviting me to read my poetry:

Invited Poet. Original Poetry. Friday Morning Book Talk Series. Osher Lifelong Learning Center. University of Missouri, Columbia. 7 June 2024.

Invited Fiction Writer. Original story. "Vulgate Psalm 39:3.5." Scissortail Creative Writing Festival. Ada, Oklahoma, 4-6 April, 2024.

Invited Poet. Original Poetry. One of four poets representing Oklahoma. Poets Building Bridges Series. Produced by Poetrybay Productions for Walt Whitman Birthplace. 9 March 2024 via Zoom.

Invited Poet. Original Poetry. Chikaskia Literary Festival. Northern Oklahoma College. Enid, OK. 5 October 2023.

Featured poet. Original Poetry. Jim Spurr's Third Thursday Series. Shawnee, Oklahoma, 20 July 2023.

Invited Poet. Original Poetry. Woody Guthrie Poets. Woody Guthrie Center. Tulsa, Oklahoma. 16 July 2023.

Invited Poet. Original Poetry. Chikaskia Literary Festival. Northern Oklahoma College. Enid, OK. 20 October 2023.

Invited Poet. Original Poetry. Woody Guthrie Poets. Woody Guthrie Center, Tulsa, Oklahoma 17 July 2022.

Invited Poet. Original Poetry. "Watermarks: Only Visible in the Light." Scissortail Creative Writing Festival. Ada, Oklahoma, 6-8 April 2023.

Featured Writer. Original Short Story from *Contrary Qualities of Elements* collection. Tidewater Second Sunday Series. Drumright, Oklahoma, 2 April, 2023.

Invited Poet. Original Poetry. "Contrary Qualities of Elements." Scissortail Creative Writing Festival. Ada, Oklahoma, 31 March-2 April 2022.

Featured Poet. Original Poetry. Lost Street Poetry Reading Series. Durant, Oklahoma, 20 March 2022.

Featured Poet. Original Poetry. Full Circle Books Readings. Oklahoma City, Oklahoma, 30 January 2022)

Featured Writer. Original Short Story. Fine Dog Press Authors Reading. Okmulgee, Oklahoma, 12 November 2021.
Featured Poet. Original Poetry. Jim Spurr's Third Thursday Series. Shawnee, Oklahoma, 21 October 2021.

Featured Poet. Original Poetry. Third Saturday Reading Series. Lawton, Oklahoma, 16 October 2021.

Featured Poet. Original Poetry. Tidewater Second Sunday Series. Drumright, Oklahoma, 10 October 2021.

Invited Poet. Original Poetry. Chikaskia Literary Festival. Tonkawa, Oklahoma, 8-9 October 2021.

Featured Poet. Original Poetry. Funky Hair Ranch Third Saturday Reading Series. Edmond, OK, 18 September 2021.

About the author

Before retiring from academic life in May 2018, Julie Chappell published six books of scholarship and a collection of her original poetry, *Faultlines: One Woman's Shifting Boundaries* (Village Books Press, 2013). Since retiring, she has published two more collections of poetry—*Mad Habits of a Life* (Lamar University Literary Press, 2019), which was nominated for the Paterson Prize in 2020, and *As I Pirouette Away* (Turning Plow Press, 2021). *Watermarks* is her fourth collection of poetry. Additionally, she has penned two collections of short stories— *Homecoming and Other Mythic Tales* (Fine Dog Press, 2021) and *Contrary Qualities of Elements* (Fine Dog Press, 2023). In March 2024, she read as one of four representatives of Oklahoma poets for a worldwide poetry Zoom created for Poets Building Bridges, hosted by George Wallace and the Walt Whitman Birthplace. In progress are a memoir, *The Jail/house Rocked 1957-1960*, and a scholarly tome entitled, *Nuns on the Run: The Dissolution of Women's Lives, 1536-1540*. She lives on Lake Keystone in northeastern Oklahoma with her poet husband, Hank Jones, and their five cats.